ENVIRONMENTAL PROTECTION AGENCY LIBRARY NETWORK

Environmental Protection Agency Library Network

Bernard T. Vellios
Editor

Nova Science Publishers, Inc.
New York

For permission to use material from this book please contact us:
Telephone 631-231-7269; Fax 631-231-8175
Web Site: http://www.novapublishers.com

LIBRARY OF CONGRESS CATALOGING-IN-PUBLICATION DATA
Available upon request
ISBN: 978-1-60692-059-6

Published by Nova Science Publishers, Inc. ✢ New York

CONTENTS

PREFACE

Environmental Protection Agency's (EPA) library network provides staff and the public with access to environmental information. Its 26 libraries contain a wide range of information and resources and are located at headquarters, regional offices, research centers, and laboratories nationwide. In 2006, EPA issued a plan to reorganize the network beginning in fiscal year 2007. The plan proposed closing libraries and dispersing, disposing of, and digitizing library materials.

GAO was asked to assess (1) the status of, and plans for, the network reorganization; (2) EPA's rationale for reorganizing the network; (3) the extent to which EPA has communicated with and solicited the views of EPA staff and external stakeholders in conducting the reorganization; (4) EPA's steps to maintain the quality of library services after the reorganization; and (5) how EPA is funding the network and its reorganization. For this study, GAO reviewed pertinent EPA documents and interviewed EPA officials and staff from each of the libraries.

In: Environmental Protection Agency... ISBN: 978-1-60692-059-6
Editor: B. T. Vellios, pp. 1-5

WHY GAO DID THIS STUDY*

Established in 1971, the Environmental Protection Agency's (EPA) library network provides staff and the public with access to environmental information. Its 26 libraries contain a wide range of information and resources and are located at headquarters, regional offices, research centers, and laboratories nationwide. In 2006, EPA issued a plan to reorganize the network beginning in fiscal year 2007. The plan proposed closing libraries and dispersing, disposing of, and digitizing library materials.

GAO was asked to assess (1) the status of, and plans for, the network reorganization; (2) EPA's rationale for reorganizing the network; (3) the extent to which EPA has communicated with and solicited the views of EPA staff and external stakeholders in conducting the reorganization; (4) EPA's steps to maintain the quality of library services after the reorganization; and (5) how EPA is funding the network and its reorganization. For this study, GAO reviewed pertinent EPA documents and interviewed EPA officials and staff from each of the libraries.

WHAT GAO RECOMMENDS

GAO recommends that EPA continue its moratorium until it takes corrective actions to (1) justify its decision to reorganize the network, (2) improve its outreach efforts, (3) ensure sufficient oversight and monitoring of the reorganization, and (4) implement procedures for the proper dispersal and disposal of library materials. EPA agreed with GAO's recommendations.

---

* Excerpted from GAO Report GAO-08-304, dated February 2008.

What GAO Found

Since 2006, EPA has implemented its reorganization plan to close physical access to 4 libraries. In the same period, 6 other libraries in the network decided to change their operations, while 16 have not changed. Some of these libraries have also digitized, dispersed, or disposed of their materials. Since the reorganization, EPA has begun drafting a common set of agencywide library procedures and has hired a program manager for the network. While these procedures are under development, however, EPA has imposed a moratorium on further changes to the network in response to congressional and other expressions of concern.

EPA's primary rationale for the library network reorganization was to generate cost savings by creating a more coordinated library network and increasing the electronic delivery of services. However, EPA did not fully follow procedures recommended in a 2004 EPA study of steps that should be taken to prepare for a reorganization. In particular, EPA did not fully evaluate alternative models, and associated costs and benefits, of library services. EPA officials stated that they needed to act quickly to reorganize the library network in response to a proposed fiscal year 2007 funding reduction.

EPA did not develop procedures to inform staff and the public on the final configuration of the library network, and EPA libraries varied considerably and were limited in the extent to which they communicated with and solicited views from stakeholders before and during the reorganization effort. In particular, EPA's plan did not include information that the Chemical Library was to close, and EPA did not inform staff or the public until after the fact. EPA's communication procedures were limited or inconsistent because EPA acted quickly to make changes in response to a proposed fiscal year 2007 funding reduction, and because of the decentralized nature of the library network. EPA is currently increasing its communication efforts.

EPA does not have a post-reorganization strategy to ensure the continuity of library services and has not yet determinedthe full effect of the reorganization on library services. Moreover, EPA has recently made several changes that could have impaired user access to library materials and services. For example, EPA did not determine whether federal property management regulations applied to the dispersal and disposal of library materials before it closed the libraries. Furthermore, EPA lacked oversight of the reorganization process and does not have procedures that would allow the agency to measure performance and monitor user needs.

Several different EPA offices are responsible for the libraries in the network. Each office generally decides how much funding to allocate to the libraries for which it is responsible and how to fund their reorganization. However, when faced with a proposed budget reduction of $2 million in fiscal year 2007, EPA specifically directed that these offices reduce funding for their libraries and did not specify how to achieve the reduction. Additional funds were not allocated to assist offices in closing their libraries.

ABBREVIATIONS

EPA	Environmental Protection Agency
GSA	General Services Administration
NEPIS	National Environmental Publications Internet Site
OARM	Office of Administration and Resources Management
OEI	Office of Environmental Information
OLS	Online Library System
OPPTS	Office of Prevention, Pesticides, and Toxic Substances
ORD	Office of Research and Development

February 29, 2008

Congressional Requesters

The Environmental Protection Agency's (EPA) library network provides access to critical environmental information that the agency needs to promote environmental awareness, conduct research, enforce environmental laws, make policy decisions, and fulfill its mission of protecting human health and the environment. In fiscal year 2006, the network included 26 libraries across headquarters, regional offices, research centers, and laboratories that were independently operated by several different EPA program offices, depending on the nature of the libraries' collections.[1] The combined network collection contains information on a spectrum of issues, including environmental protection and management, sciences, legislative mandates on environmental matters, and specialized regional or program office topics. The network provides this information and research support to assist EPA staff in performing their work. EPA enforcement staff, for example, use the libraries to obtain scientific and technical information to support the development of enforcement cases and to conduct research on legal and business issues. The library network also provides information and services to state environmental agencies, local community organizations, and the general public to help these stakeholders in protecting human health and the environment.

In fiscal year 2007, EPA began to reorganize its library network on the basis of a 2006 reorganization plan issued by EPA's Office of Environmental Information (OEI) that focused on its headquarters library and the 10 regional office libraries. In addition to these 11 libraries, the network included 15 libraries located in EPA laboratories or in other EPA program offices, such as the Office of Prevention, Pesticides, and Toxic Substances (OPPTS). Funding for the OEI headquarters and regional office libraries account for about 36 percent of the funding spent on library activities in fiscal year 2006. The 2006 plan—*EPA FY 2007 Library Plan: National Framework for the Headquarters and Regional Libraries*—and the reorganization were accelerated by a proposed $2 million budget reduction for the OEI libraries based on the President's fiscal year 2007 budget request.[2] The plan was intended to provide a framework on how to consolidate libraries and make more materials and services available online. As such, the plan proposed a phased approach to closing physical access to some libraries and the creation of Library Centers of Excellence to provide library services on specific issue areas, while continuing to ensure access to library services and information for EPA staff and the public.[3] It stated that 3 regional libraries, located in Chicago, Dallas, and Kansas City, would close and that their collections would be dispersed to other EPA or non-EPA libraries, disposed of, or digitized and made available online. The plan also proposed that a headquarters library, managed by OEI, would close physical access but would serve as one of EPA's three repositories for storing EPA's hard copy collections.[4] Under the plan, EPA staff and the public would not have walk-in access to collections at the closed headquarters or regional office libraries, but they would continue to have access to reports and documents electronically or hard copy access via interlibrary loan. EPA staff would also be able to obtain research and reference assistance from librarians provided by their library or by a Center of Excellence through a service agreement.

With the reorganization of the EPA library network, Congress, professional library associations, and others have raised concerns regarding how such changes will affect the delivery of information that is critical to fulfilling EPA's mission. In general, their concerns focus on several procedural aspects of the reorganization effort. These include the closing of libraries or reducing their hours of operation; the rationale for reorganizing the library network in the first place; the procedures used in dispersing, disposing of, and digitizing library materials; steps being taken to guard against potential degradation of library services; and the availability of resources to enable the libraries to continue meeting their missions.

In this context, you asked us to obtain and analyze information relevant to these concerns. Specifically, you asked that we (1) determine the status of, and plans for, the library network reorganization; (2) evaluate EPA's rationale for its decision to reorganize the library network; (3) assess the extent to which EPA has communicated with and solicited views from EPA staff and external stakeholders in planning and implementing the reorganization; (4) evaluate the steps EPA has taken to maintain the quality of library services following the reorganization, both currently and in the future; and (5) determine how EPA is funding the library network and its reorganization.

To address these objectives, we reviewed relevant EPA documents, policies, plans, and guidance as well as related laws and requirements pertinent to the library network and reorganization effort. To determine key practices for change management, we assessed EPA's reorganization effort against our past work on key practices and implementation steps to assist mergers and organizational transformations.[5] We interviewed EPA librarians and library managers from each of the 26 libraries in EPA's library network as well as EPA officials knowledgeable about EPA's library network and budget. In addition, we interviewed representatives from local unions, who represent EPA staff, and regional science councils, which is a group that consists of EPA scientists and technical specialists. We also sought information from library professionals, including representatives from the American Library Association and the Association of Research Libraries; members of academia; and private consulting companies with expertise in libraries. Appendix I provides a detailed discussion of our objectives, scope, and methodology.

We conducted this performance audit from December 2006 through February 2008 in accordance with generally accepted government auditing standards. Those standards require that we plan and perform the audit to obtain sufficient, appropriate evidence to provide a reasonable basis for our findings and conclusions based on our audit objectives. We believe that the evidence obtained provides a reasonable basis for our findings and conclusions based on our audit objectives.

In: Environmental Protection Agency...
Editor: B. T. Vellios, pp. 7-10
ISBN: 978-1-60692-059-6

Chapter 1

RESULTS IN BRIEF

Since 2006, EPA has implemented its library reorganization plan to close physical access to the OEI headquarters library and 3 regional office libraries. In the same period, 6 other libraries in the network independently decided to change their operations: 1 closed, 4 reduced their hours of operation, and 1 changed the way it provides library services. Sixteen libraries have not changed. Furthermore, some of these libraries have digitized, dispersed, or disposed of their materials. The reorganization effort has largely been decentralized: that is, the EPA program or regional office responsible for each library independently decided what types of changes to make. Since implementing the reorganization, EPA has begun drafting a common set of agencywide library procedures and has hired a program manager for the library network. While these procedures are under development, however, EPA has imposed a moratorium on further changes to the library network in response to congressional and other concerns. EPA officials told us that the agency wants to refine its library procedures, among other things, before lifting the moratorium, but it has not set a date for completing these refinements. The future of the library network, its configuration, and its operations may be contingent on (1) the completion of its library procedures; (2) EPA's response to directions accompanying its fiscal year 2008 appropriation to use $1 million to restore libraries recently closed; and (3) EPA's 2008 library plan, which describes how EPA expects to operate the library network in the future. At the time of our review, EPA was drafting its 2008 library plan and had not yet submitted a report to the Senate and House Committees on Appropriations on how the agency will restore the EPA library network per the fiscal year 2008 appropriations act.

EPA's primary rationale for reorganizing its library network was to generate cost savings by creating a more coordinated library network and increasing the electronic delivery of services. However, EPA did not effectively justify its decision to reorganize the library network because it did not implement a process for conducting a number of analyses, including many that were recommended in its own study of the libraries prior to initiating the reorganization. According to this 2004 internal study, the library network was generally cost-effective but could be improved with a reorganization that followed certain recommended actions. To make a more informed decision on how best to reorganize, the study recommended that EPA first, among other things, survey EPA staff who use the libraries, review and revise the policy and procedures that guide the library network, and develop and review alternative models of library services. However, EPA did not fully implement these steps. In addition, Office of Management and Budget guidance recommends that agencies conduct a benefit-cost analysis to support decisions to initiate, renew, or expand programs or projects, and that, in conducting such an analysis, tangible and intangible benefits and costs be identified, assessed, and reported. However, EPA did not perform a benefit-cost analysis in this case. According to EPA officials, OEI decided to reorganize its libraries without completing the recommended analyses because it wanted to reduce its fiscal year 2007 funding by $2 million to create the savings necessary for its headquarters library and the regional office libraries per the President's budget proposal.

EPA did not develop procedures to inform the full range of stakeholders on the final configuration of the library network, and EPA libraries varied considerably in the extent to which they communicated with and solicited views from staff, external stakeholders, and experts before and during the reorganization. Such efforts were limited or inconsistent because EPA acted quickly to make changes in response to a proposed fiscal year 2007 funding reduction and because of the decentralized nature of the library network. As we have previously reported,[6] an organization's transformation or merger is strengthened when it sets and makes public implementation goals and an outline; establishes a communication strategy by communicating early and often to build trust, ensuring consistency of message, and involving staff to obtain their ideas and gain ownership for the transformation; and adopts leading practices to build a world-class organization. In the case of the library network reorganization, EPA did not do the following:

1 Inform stakeholders on how the final library network would be configured or the implementation goals and timeline that it would take to achieve this final configuration. For example, EPA's library plan did not include information that the Chemical Library was to close, and EPA did

not inform staff or the public that the library was to close until after the fact. The lack of transparency in the reorganization process could result in a lack of support for the effort.

2 Have an agencywide communication strategy for the reorganization effort and, as a result, did not conduct outreach activities consistently across libraries or conducted them in a limited fashion. For example, only a few of the regional libraries solicited staff views through discussions with union representatives. EPA also did not generally solicit the views of the public and library associations. Without an agencywide communication strategy, staff ownership for the changes may be limited, staff may be confused about the changes, and EPA cannot be sure the changes are meeting the needs of EPA staff and external stakeholders.

3 Solicit views from experts to obtain information on leading practices for library services. As such, EPA cannot be sure that it is using leading practices in its effort to reorganize the network.

EPA officials are currently reaching out to stakeholders, including EPA staff and library experts, by holding and attending stakeholder meetings and conferences.

EPA does not have an effective strategy to ensure the continuity of library services following the reorganization and does not know the full effect of the reorganization on library services. According to our review of key practices and implementation steps to assist mergers and organizational transformations, organizations that are undergoing change should seek and monitor staff attitudes and take appropriate follow-up actions. EPA's library plan describes the reorganization effort as a "phased approach," but it does not provide specific goals, timelines, or feedback mechanisms that allow the agency to measure performance and monitor user needs to ensure a successful reorganization while maintaining quality services. To balance the continued delivery of services with merger or transformation activities, we have also found that it is essential to ensure that top leadership drives the transformation. However, EPA lacked a national program manager for the library network to oversee and guide the reorganization effort, and each library decided whether to close and how to disperse and dispose of library materials. EPA did not choose to follow such key practices for a successful transformation, even though the agency made several changes to the library network that could have impaired the continued delivery of library materials and services to its staff and the public. For example, service agreements were not fully tested in advance to determine their effectiveness. Furthermore, EPA did not determine whether federal property management regulations applied to the dispersal and disposal of library materials before it closed the libraries.

In the absence of such a determination, EPA provided vague criteria and guidance to its libraries without adequately overseeing the process.

The several different program offices responsible for the EPA libraries in the network each decide how much of their available funding to allocate to their libraries and how to fund their reorganization. For example, OEI typically provides funding for the regional office libraries through each region's support budget, and gives regional management discretion on how to allocate this funding among the library and other support services on the basis of the needs and priorities in the region. However, when faced with a proposed budget reduction of $2 million in fiscal year 2007, rather than following its normal procedures by giving regional office and headquarters managers discretion on how to allocate their budgets, OEI specifically directed the regional and headquarters offices to reduce funding for OEI libraries—a reduction of 77 percent for these libraries from the previous fiscal year. EPA did not specifically allocate funds to help closing libraries manage their collections; instead, the program or regional office responsible for the libraries used its annual funding to pay for these costs. Services formerly provided by the closed libraries are now provided on a fee-for-service basis by other libraries in the network. Regarding the costs of the reorganization, OEI and OPPTS did not track the costs associated with closing the libraries, such as boxing, shipping, and digitizing materials. However, EPA estimated that it spent about $80,000 to digitize 15,260 titles between December 2006 and January 2007. This effort was funded by the Office of Administration and Resources Management (OARM) under an already existing contract.

In light of these findings, we are recommending that the Administrator of EPA continue the agency's moratorium on changes to the library network until the agency (1) develops a strategy to justify its reorganization plans; (2) improves its outreach efforts; (3) ensures sufficient oversight and control over the reorganization process, and continuously and consistently monitors the impact of the reorganization on EPA staff and the public; and (4) implements procedures ensuring that library materials are dispersed and disposed of consistently and in accordance with federal property management regulations.

In: Environmental Protection Agency…
Editor: B. T. Vellios, pp. 11-16
ISBN: 978-1-60692-059-6

Chapter 2

BACKGROUND

Soon after the creation of EPA, the library network was formed to provide staff and the public with access to environmental information in support of EPA's mission to protect human health and the environment. Established in 1971, the network is composed of libraries and repositories located in the agency's headquarters, regional offices, research centers, and laboratories throughout the country. The combined network collection contains a wide range of general information on environmental protection and management; basic and applied sciences, such as biology, chemistry, engineering, and toxicology; and extensive coverage of topics featured in legislative mandates, such as hazardous waste, drinking water, pollution prevention, and toxic substances. Several of the libraries maintain collections that are focused on special topics to support specific regional or program office projects. As such, the libraries differ in function, scope of collections, extent of services, and public access.

During this period, EPA's library network operations were guided by EPA's *Information Resources Management Policy Manual*. Chapter 12 of the policy manual stipulated that the library network provide EPA staff with access to information to carry out the agency's mission, and that the libraries provide state agencies and the public with access to the library collection. Chapter 12 also established the role of the national program manager with responsibility for coordinating major activities of the EPA library network. A national program manager within OEI is responsible for coordinating the major activities of the EPA library network. The role of the national program manager is to work with the library network and its managers to provide several essential services, such as assessing the needs of program staff and providing services to meet those needs.

Unlike other national program manager positions at EPA, the national program manager for the library network does not have budget authority for the libraries.

Before the 2007 reorganization, 26 libraries comprised the library network, each funded and managed by several different program offices at EPA:[7] 1 library was managed by OEI, 10 libraries were managed by regional offices,[8] 8 libraries were located at EPA laboratories within the Office of Research and Development (ORD), and 2 libraries were located within OARM. In addition, each of the following program offices had 1 library: Office of the Administrator, Office of General Counsel, OPPTS, Office of Enforcement and Compliance Assurance, and Office of Air and Radiation.

In addition to its physical locations and holdings, the EPA network provides access to its collections through a Web-based database of library holdings—the Online Library System (OLS)—that is known as EPA's online "card catalog." OLS enables EPA staff and the public to search for materials in any of the EPA libraries across the country that are part of the network. According to EPA estimates, the combined EPA collection in 2003 included 504,000 books and reports; 3,500 journals; 25,000 maps; and 3,600,000 information objects on microfilm. If an item is not available on-site to EPA staff or the public, it is made available through interlibrary loan from another library within the network or another public library. Up to 26,000 of these EPA documents are available electronically to EPA staff and the public through a separate online database—the National Environmental Publications Internet Site (NEPIS). In addition, EPA staff have access to over 120,000 information sources—such as online journals, the *Federal Register*, news, databases of bibliographic information, and article citations—from their desktop computers.

Librarians are available to assist EPA staff and the public, and, as of March 2007, professional librarian staff accounted for just over 36 full-time-equivalent employees. In addition to these 6 federal librarians and 30 contract librarians, several other staff, such as technical specialists and library technicians, also work at the libraries. Library staff provide a number of services to both EPA staff and the public, including (1) support for EPA scientists and technical staff, such as responding to quick and extended reference questions, conducting literature and database searches, and providing training to EPA staff on how to conduct their own searches; (2) support for EPA enforcement staff, such as conducting legal or business research and providing scientific and technical information to support enforcement cases; (3) collection cataloging and maintenance; and (4) support for the general public, such as answering quick and extended reference questions, and providing training on how to search EPA databases. In fiscal year 2005, the services provided to EPA staff by librarians at OEI headquarters and regional office libraries included 41,029 quick and extended reference checks, 8,286 interlibrary loans, and 85,226 database and literature searches. These librarians also provided EPA staff with 52,975 resources, such as books and journal articles.

Beginning in 2003, EPA conducted a business case assessment of its library network and a study of options for future regional library operations. These two studies,[9] which primarily focused on the OEI headquarters library and the regional office libraries, were intended to determine the value of library services and inform management in the regions of their options to support library services beyond fiscal year 2006. In August 2005, regional management formed a Library Network Workgroup, composed of regional and headquarters library managers as well as library managers from OARM and the National Environmental Investigations Center libraries, to review the two reports and develop recommendations on ways to maintain an effective library network if the library support budget were reduced. The workgroup issued its internal report, *EPA Library Network: Challenges for FY 2007 and Beyond*, in November 2005.

After the Library Network Workgroup's report was issued, EPA established a Library Steering Committee, composed of senior managers from EPA's program offices and regions, to develop a new model for providing library services to EPA staff. As such, the steering committee reviewed the recommendations made by the workgroup and, in August 2006, issued the *EPA FY 2007 Library Plan: National Framework for the Headquarters and Regional Libraries*. See figure 1 for a timeline of the assessments and planning efforts that EPA conducted and library network reorganization activities.

The August 2006 library plan provided the framework for the network to begin reorganizing in the summer of 2006 in preparation for the proposed fiscal year 2007 budget reduction beginning in October 2006. (In September 2004, a Region 2 laboratory library in Edison, New Jersey, closed, and a Region 3 laboratory library in Fort Meade, Maryland, closed access to the public in February 2006.) The plan describes a "phased approach" to disperse and dispose of library materials in the libraries that will close. The plan also provided guidelines for EPA staff to determine how the collections are to be managed. According to the plan, OEI libraries in Regions 5, 6, and 7 would close and the headquarters library would close physical access to its collection but would function as one of three repository libraries. OARM libraries located in Cincinnati, Ohio, and Research Triangle Park, North Carolina, would serve as the other two repositories. In addition, according to the plan, EPA is developing Library Centers of Excellence, where a library with more expertise in a specific area of reference research would provide that service to staff in other regions.

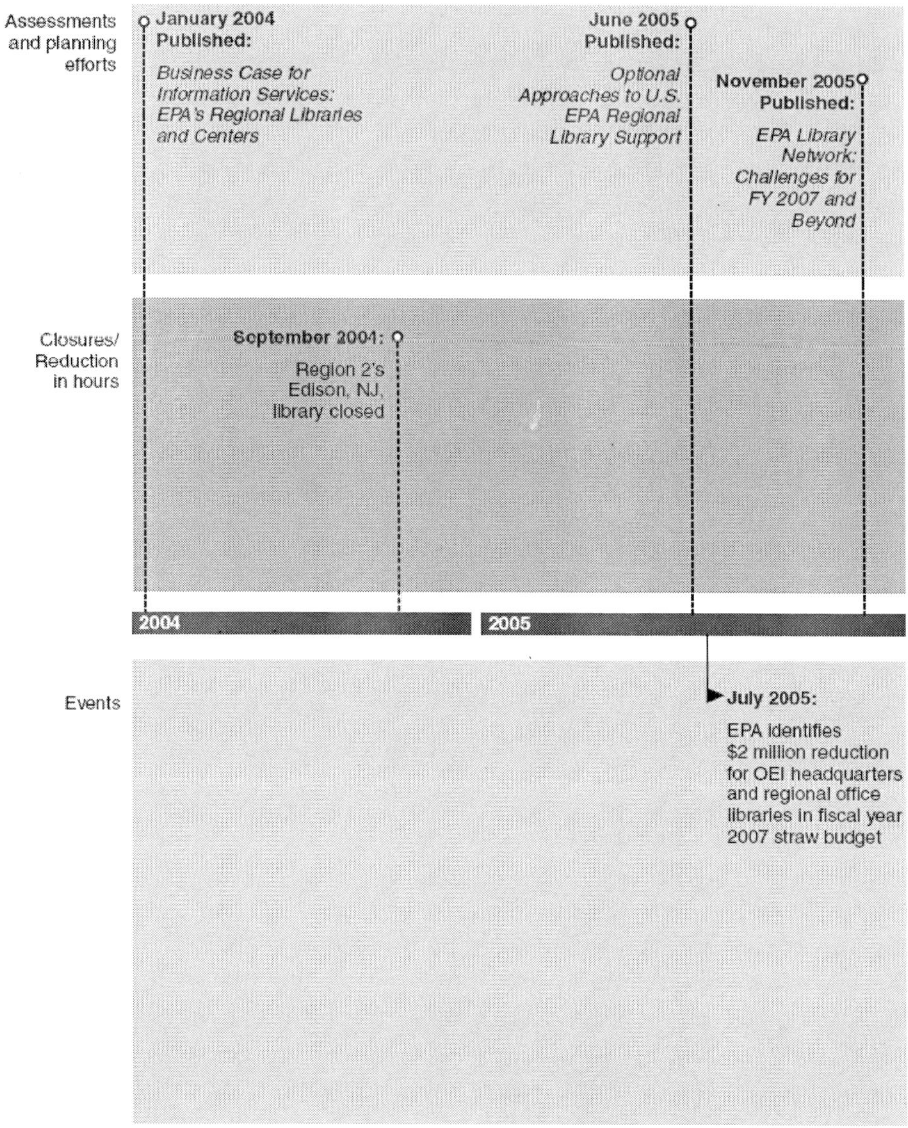

Assessments and planning efforts
January 2004 Published:
Business Case for Information Services: EPA's Regional Libraries and Centers
June 2005 Published:
Optional Approaches to U.S. EPA Regional Library Support
November 2005 Published:
EPA Library Network: Challenges for FY 2007 and Beyond
Closures/ Reduction in hours
September 2004:
Region 2's Edison, NJ, library closed
2004
2005
Events
July 2005:
EPA identifies $2 million reduction for OEI headquarters and regional office libraries in fiscal year 2007 straw budget

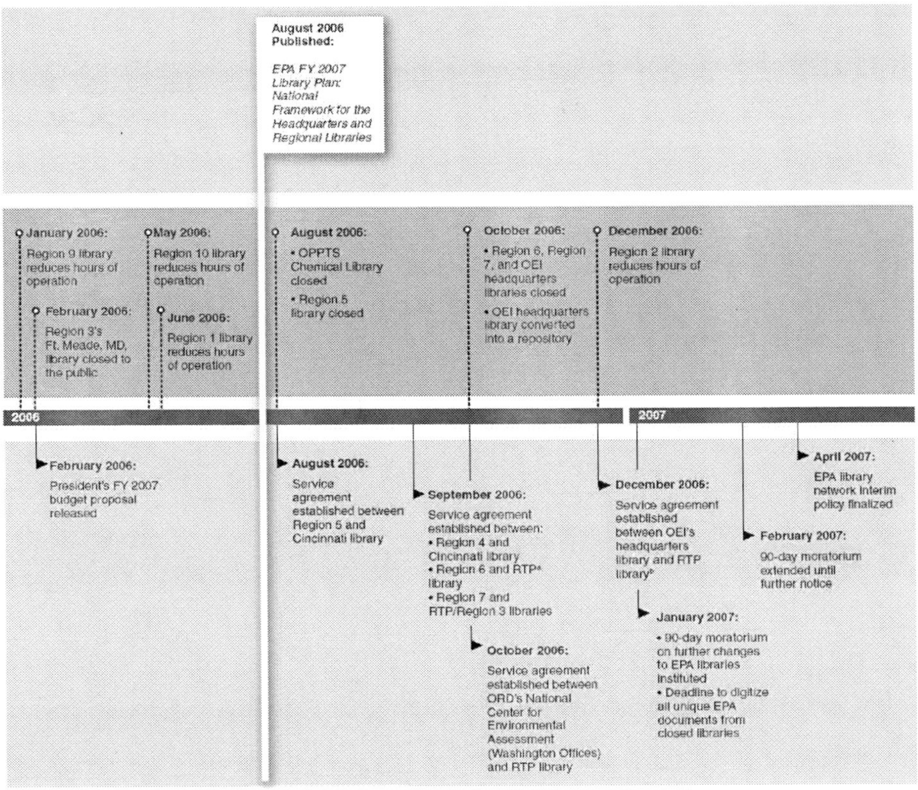

Source: GAO analysis of EPA data.

[a]"RTP" denotes Research Triangle Park, North Carolina.

[b]This service agreement, according to OPPTS officials, also provides services to OPPTS and other EPA staff affected by the closure of the Chemical Library.

Figure 1. Timeline of EPA Library Network Assessments and Planning Efforts and Reorganization Activities.

Members of Congress and congressional committees, library professional associations, public interest groups, and individuals have expressed several concerns about the reorganization of the library network. Specifically:

- During the reorganization, several Members of Congress submitted letters to EPA and to the President asking to restore funding or asking for specific information regarding the reorganization.
- In a February 2006 letter, representatives of 4 library associations asked the House Committee on Appropriations to restore the budget cuts to the

library network and to require EPA to develop an information management strategy.

- In a June 2006 letter, the presidents of 16 local unions, representing over 10,000 EPA scientists, engineers, and environmental protection specialists, protested the budget cut to the library network to the Senate Committee on Appropriations.
- In August 2006, the American Federation of Government Employees National Council of EPA Locals filed a formal grievance, requesting that negotiations be held with the union regarding the library network reorganization.[10]

In: Environmental Protection Agency...
Editor: B. T. Vellios, pp. 17-26
ISBN: 978-1-60692-059-6

Chapter 3

SOME LIBRARIES INDEPENDENTLY DECIDED TO CLOSE, REDUCE THEIR HOURS, OR TAKE OTHER ACTIONS, BUT THE FINAL NETWORK CONFIGURATION IS STILL UNCERTAIN

As a part of EPA's 2006 reorganization effort, some EPA libraries have closed, reduced their hours of operation, or changed the way that they provide library services. Furthermore, some of these libraries have digitized, dispersed, or disposed of their materials. As noted in EPA's August 2006 library plan, 1 OEI headquarters library closed and 3 regional office libraries closed; but during the same period, 6 other libraries in the network independently decided to change their operations—1 closed, 4 reduced their hours of operation, and 1 changed the way that it provides library services. Sixteen EPA libraries have not changed. During the reorganization effort, each of the libraries in the network made its own decision on how it would manage its collection—some digitized, or have plans to digitize, some of their materials; some dispersed their materials to EPA and non-EPA libraries; and some disposed of their materials. After making these changes, EPA has begun to develop a common set of agencywide policies and procedures for the library network. EPA is waiting to complete these policies and procedures before lifting a moratorium on further change. The future of EPA's library network—its configuration and its operations—are contingent on the final policies and procedures, on EPA's response to directions accompanying its fiscal year 2008 appropriation, and on EPA's 2008 library plan.

Some Libraries Independently Decided to Close, and Others Reduced Their Hours or Changed the Way that They Provided Library Services

Due to the decentralized nature of the EPA library network, each library decided on its own whether to close, reduce hours of operation, change the way that it provided library services, or make no changes in order to prepare for a proposed budget reduction. As table 1 shows, 4 libraries—as noted in EPA's library plan—closed physical access to their libraries. Furthermore, 1 additional library in the network closed, 4 reduced their hours of operation, and 1 changed the way that it provides library services. However, these changes were not noted in EPA's library reorganization plan. Sixteen libraries in the network did not institute any changes.

Table 1. Operating Status of Each Library in the EPA Library Network

Program office	Library/Location	Operating status of library
Office of Environmental Information	Headquarters Library/Washington, DC	Closed physical access
		Serves as a repository library
Regional Office	Region 1 Library/Boston, MA	Reduced hours of operation
	Region 2 Library/New York, NY	Reduced hours of operation[a]
	Region 3 Library/Philadelphia, PA	Open[b]
	Region 4 Library/Atlanta, GA	Open
		Changed the way that library services are provided
	Region 5 Library/Chicago, IL	Closed physical access[c]
	Region 6 Library/Dallas, TX	Closed physical access[c, d]
	Region 7 Library/Kansas City, KS	Closed physical access[d]
	Region 8 Library/Denver, CO	Open
	Region 9 Library/San Francisco, CA	Reduced hours of operation
	Region 10 Library/Seattle, WA	Reduced hours of operation
Office of Prevention, Pesticides, and Toxic Substances	Chemical Library/Washington, DC	Closed physical access[c]
Office of Administration and Resources Management	Andrew Breidenbach Environmental Research Center/Cincinnati, OH	Open Serves as a repository library

Program office	Library/Location	Operating status of library
	Research Triangle Park Library Service/Research	Open
	Triangle Park, NC	Serves as a repository library
Office of Enforcement and Compliance Assurance	National Enforcement Investigations Center Environmental Forensics Library/Denver, CO	Open
Office of Research and Development	Environmental Sciences Division Technical Research Center/Las Vegas, NV	Open
	Ecosystem Research Division Library/Athens, GA	Open
	Atlantic Ecology Division Library/Narragansett, RI	Open
	Gulf Ecology Division Library/Gulf Breeze, FL	Open
	Mid-continent Ecology Division Library/Duluth, MN	Open
	Western Ecology Division Library/Corvallis, OR	Open
	Ground Water and Ecosystems Restoration	Open
	Division Library/Ada, OK	
	Atmospheric Sciences Modeling Division Library/	Open[e]
	Research Triangle Park, NC	
Office of the Administrator	Legislative Reference Library/Washington, DC	Open
Office of General Counsel	Law Library/Washington, DC	Open
Office of Air and Radiation	National Vehicle and Fuel Emissions Laboratory	Open
	Library/Ann Arbor, MI	

[a]A library located at an Edison, New Jersey, laboratory in Region 2 closed in September 2004. This library closure preceded the closures associated with the fiscal year 2007 library network reorganization. Although this library was managed separately and independently from the Region 2 library, the materials from this library were transferred to the main Region 2 library in New York, New York, when the library closed. Librarians from the main library in Region 2 now provide library services to Edison, New Jersey, staff.

[b]The lone librarian in Region 3's satellite library in Ft. Meade, Maryland, resigned in February 2006. The Ft. Meade library's collection remains in place and is open for EPA staff use, although no staff manage the collection. Librarians from the main library in Region 3, located in Philadelphia, Pennsylvania, now provide library services to Ft. Meade staff. According to EPA officials, the Ft. Meade library was closed to the public because the library did not receive many visits from the public, and because the library was located at a high-security military base.

[c]The libraries in Regions 5 and 6 and the Chemical Library reduced their hours of operation for a period of time prior to closing.

[d]The libraries in Regions 6 and 7, although closed to physical access, still contain library materials on shelves because of the moratorium on further changes to the network that was placed in January 2007. According to EPA officials, materials from the Regions 6 and 7 libraries are not accessible to walk-in traffic but remain accessible through interlibrary loan.

[e]The Atmospheric Sciences Modeling Division library was funded by the National Oceanic and Atmospheric Administration but run jointly by ORD through an interagency agreement. The library materials for this library are located at Research Triangle Park, North Carolina, and managed by OARM library staff. In fiscal year 2008, the library was not funded and will be consolidated into the OARM Research Triangle Park library once the moratorium is lifted, according to EPA officials.

Source: GAO analysis of EPA data.

EPA's August 2006 library plan notes that three regional libraries—Regions 5 (Chicago), 6 (Dallas), and 7 (Kansas City)—and the headquarters library in Washington, D.C., would close physical access to their libraries. In addition, OPPTS officials decided to close the Chemical Library; however, this closure was not noted in the plan. According to EPA officials, the plan focused on the OEI headquarters and regional office libraries, and they did not think it was necessary to reflect changes that were planned for other libraries. The focus of the plan, according to EPA officials, was to set the framework on how library services would be provided electronically and not on what physical changes in the network were to occur. Although no longer accessible to walk-in traffic from EPA staff and the public, the closed regional and headquarters libraries continue to provide library services, such as interlibrary loans and research/reference requests, to EPA staff through service agreements that the closed libraries established with libraries managed by OARM—located in Cincinnati, Ohio, or Research Triangle Park, North Carolina—or with the Region 3 library located in Philadelphia, Pennsylvania.[11] Service agreements have been established between (1) the Cincinnati library and Region 5, (2) the Research Triangle Park library and headquarters as well as Regions 6 and 7, and (3) Region 3 and Region 7.[12] According to OPPTS officials, library services are provided to OPPTS staff through a service agreement that the headquarters library has established with the Research Triangle Park library, although OPPTS is not a signatory to the service agreement. The library plan noted that the public would access materials previously held by the closed regional and headquarters libraries, either electronically using NEPIS, a database of electronic EPA publications, or physically using interlibrary loan.

For the regional libraries that had closed, their library spaces remain unused. The Region 5 library space is empty, with all of its shelving and furniture sold through a General Services Administration (GSA) auction for $327. According to Region 5 officials, the space is occasionally used for meetings, but no plans have been made on how the space will be used. Many of the library materials remain on shelves in Regions 6 and 7 because of the moratorium. According to a Region 7 official, because the library space is not being maintained, some of its shelving has been removed and used for other purposes. EPA officials noted that they plan to use the headquarters and Chemical Library spaces for the headquarters repository, which would house repository materials and the Chemical Library collection (see fig. 2 for a photograph of boxed-up books from the Region 5 library, now located at the headquarters repository library). However, the library space in the Chemical Library is currently being used as office space, although nearly half of the space is devoted to shelving that cannot be removed because it is considered historical.

Source: GAO.

Figure 2. Boxed-up Books from the Region 5 Library Now on Shelves in the Headquarters Repository Library.

Of the four regional libraries that decided to reduce their hours of operation, Regions 9 and 10 reduced their hours by about 30 percent, and Regions 1 and 2 reduced their hours by more than 50 percent. The library plan did not note that these libraries would be reducing their hours. As we have previously noted, the focus of the plan, according to EPA officials, was to set the framework on how library services would be provided electronically and not on what physical changes in the network were to occur. As such, EPA officials stated that they did not think it was necessary to list in the plan which libraries were planning on reducing hours.

Also, as noted in table 1, the Region 4 library changed the way that it provided library services to its regional staff. While the library is accessible to EPA staff and the public, and materials remain in place, the library reduced the number of on-site contract librarians and established a service agreement with the OARM library in Cincinnati, Ohio, to provide Region 4 EPA staff with some core library services. These core services include interlibrary loans, cataloging, online literature searches, and reference and research requests. There is currently one full-time professional federal librarian located at the Region 4 library. The library plan did not note that Region 4 would change the way that it provides library services to its staff and the public.

Each EPA Library Independently Decided which Materials Should Be Selected for Digitization, Dispersal, or Disposal

As part of the library reorganization, each library in the network that was planning to close access to walk-in services independently decided which materials would be retained at their library or be selected for digitization, dispersal to EPA or non-EPA libraries, or disposal. To assist libraries in the regions and headquarters in determining which actions to take, OEI, in the library plan, issued general guidance and criteria as well as digitization and dispersal procedures that outlined the types of materials that could be (1) digitized and included in NEPIS or dispersed to other EPA network libraries, (2) dispersed to non-EPA libraries, and (3) disposed of or recycled. Furthermore, the guidance instructed libraries downsizing or eliminating their collections to, among other things, follow all applicable government property rules and regulations, obtain the advice of the Office of General Counsel or Regional Counsel regarding the materials needed for rulemaking or litigation purposes, consult EPA staff experts in different disciplines for their views on what to retain, review journal titles to determine if they are available online or elsewhere in the library network, and update cataloging records. Furthermore, the guidance discouraged the establishment of minilibraries. Table 2 shows the actions taken by the closed libraries.

Table 2. Current Status of Materials at Closed Libraries

Program office	Library	Digitized[a]	Dispersed to EPA or non-EPA libraries	Disposed
Office of Environmental Information	Headquarters	X	X	X
Regional Office	Region 5	X	X	
	Region 6	X	X	
	Region 7	X		
Office of Prevention, Pesticides, and Toxic Substances	Chemical Library	b	X	X

[a] In addition to the closed libraries, libraries in Regions 2 and 3, and the Atmospheric Sciences Modeling Division library in Research Triangle Park, North Carolina, also digitized materials.

[b] The OPPTS Chemical Library has developed a list of materials to be digitized but has not yet digitized any materials because of the moratorium on further changes to the library network, and because EPA's digitization procedures are undergoing third-party review. While these materials sit in boxes in the headquarters repository library and the OPPTS Chemical Library, EPA officials told us the materials can be identified and retrieved if a request arises.

Source: GAO analysis of EPA data.

In terms of digitization, the criteria in the August 2006 library plan noted that unique EPA materials—which, according to EPA officials, refers to materials created by or for EPA—that are not already electronically available in NEPIS would be digitized and made available in NEPIS. The plan indicated that these materials from libraries closing physical access would receive first priority for digitization and, according to EPA officials, set a digitization deadline for these materials by January 31, 2007. With the exception of the OPPTS Chemical Library, all of the libraries that closed digitized unique EPA materials from their library.

At the time of our review, 15,260 titles had been digitized, and EPA anticipates that about 51,000 unique EPA library materials from closed and open libraries will be digitized. OARM, in Cincinnati, was responsible for digitizing materials and dispersing the hard copy of these materials to an EPA repository or, if applicable, an originating library.[13] Some officials we talked with at libraries that have not yet digitized materials indicated that they would like to do so in the future.

In terms of dispersal, EPA's library plan noted that a library choosing to disperse its materials can do so to one of the EPA-designated repositories and other libraries in the library network, or it can transfer EPA records to EPA regional record management centers. The plan also provided guidance on what types of materials can be dispersed to the repository libraries—EPA materials that EPA staff do not use frequently and that are not available electronically, out-of-print publications, and materials that have historical significance. In addition, materials that repository libraries do not need or that other network libraries will not accept can be dispersed to, in order of preference, other federal agency libraries, state libraries and state environmental agency libraries, colleges and university libraries, public libraries, or e-mail networks used specifically to exchange library materials. The plan also noted that some materials can be dispersed to the Library of Congress and program office staff. Materials that were dispersed from the closed libraries were dispersed to other libraries within the network as well as to non-EPA libraries, including other federal agencies, state governments, universities, and private companies. No open libraries dispersed their materials as part of the reorganization effort. Table 3 shows the general location of where a majority of the dispersed materials from the closed libraries were sent.

Table 3. General Location of Most of the Dispersed Materials from Closed Libraries

Program office	Library	Location of dispersed materials
Office of Environmental Information	Headquarters	Other EPA network libraries
Regional Office	Region 5	Other EPA network libraries, other federal agencies, state governments, universities, and private companies
	Region 6	Other EPA network libraries, other federal agencies, state governments, universities, and private companies[a]
	Region 7	a
Office of Prevention, Pesticides, and Toxic Substances	Chemical Library	Other EPA network libraries

[a]Region 6 dispersed some of its materials, and Region 7 has prepared a list of materials that will be dispersed to EPA repositories. However, officials in both regions told us they were unable to move forward because of the moratorium. The materials that have not been dispersed remain on shelves in the libraries and are not directly accessible to walk-ins from EPA staff or the public.

Source: GAO analysis of EPA data.

Finally, in terms of disposal, the OEI headquarters library and the OPPTS Chemical Library disposed of some of its materials as a part of the reorganization.[14] EPA's library plan noted that materials not claimed during the dispersal process could be destroyed if they were (1) materials that are published commercially and that are outdated; (2) materials in poor physical condition, unless their content is rare or the item is the last copy in the network and is not available elsewhere electronically; and (3) microfilm of journals that are available through online archives. OPPTS officials told us that they had followed OEI's criteria and related procedures. In total, the OEI headquarters library has disposed of over 800 journals and books, and the Chemical Library has disposed of over 3,000 journals and books.

EPA Is Drafting Procedures for the Library Network, and the Network's Final Configuration Is Unknown

Recognizing that libraries could function more cohesively as a network, EPA established a new interim library policy in 2007, which superseded Chapter 12 of the *Information Resources Management Policy Manual* and established uniform governance and management for the network. This interim policy held the Assistant Administrator for Environmental Information responsible for the management of the EPA library network, including setting policy and supporting procedures, standards, and guidance to ensure effective oversight. The policy also (1) made assistant and regional administrators of network libraries responsible for complying with agencywide library policies, procedures, standards, and guidance and (2) reestablished the National Library Program Manager position, which was left vacant from 2005 through 2007, when many changes related to the reorganization occurred. This interim policy resulted in 12 draft agencywide library procedures, including procedures on digitizing and dispersing library materials, developing use statistics, providing public access, providing reference and research assistance, and developing a communication strategy. EPA officials told us that they do not have a time frame for completing these procedures but will complete them before the Chief Information Officer and Assistant Administrator of OEI lifts the moratorium on changes to the network, which was imposed in January 2007 in response to congressional and other concerns, and extended indefinitely in February 2007. The moratorium directed EPA staff to make no changes to library services, including closing libraries; reducing hours of operations, services, or resources; and dispersing and disposing of library materials.

The future of the library network, its configuration, and its operations are contingent on the completion of the final policies and procedures, on EPA's response to directions accompanying its fiscal year 2008 appropriation, and on EPA's 2008 library plan. In an explanatory statement accompanying the fiscal year 2008 Consolidated Appropriations Act, which provides funding for most federal agencies, including EPA, $1 million was allocated to restore the network of EPA libraries that were recently closed or consolidated. In addition, the explanatory statement directed EPA to submit a plan to the Committees on Appropriations within 90 days of enactment regarding actions it will take to restore the network. The act was signed by the President on December 26, 2007,[15] and EPA had not yet submitted a plan. Separately, EPA officials told us that they are working on developing a *Library Strategic Plan for 2008 and Beyond*, which details EPA's library services for staff and the public and a vision for the future of the library network.

In: Environmental Protection Agency...
Editor: B. T. Vellios, pp. 27-31
ISBN: 978-1-60692-059-6

Chapter 4

EPA DID NOT EFFECTIVELY JUSTIFY ITS DECISION TO REORGANIZE ITS LIBRARY NETWORK

EPA's primary rationale for reorganizing its library network was to generate cost savings by creating a more coordinated library network and increasing the electronic delivery of library services. However, EPA did not fully complete several analyses, including many that its 2004 study recommended. In addition, EPA's decision to reorganize its library network was not based on a thorough analyses of the costs and benefits associated with such a reorganization. Therefore, we believe that EPA's decision to reorganize the network was not fully justified.

EPA's 2004 *Business Case* report was initiated because of ongoing budget uncertainties and of changes in technology and in how users obtain information and how commercial information resources are made available. The report concluded that EPA's libraries provide "substantial value" to the agency and the public, providing benefits ranging between $2.00 and $5.70 for every $1.00 spent on the network.[16] These benefits are based on time saved in finding information with the assistance of a librarian. The calculated benefit-cost ratio varied, depending on the dollar value ascribed to time savings and the type of service provided. The report also noted other unquantifiable benefits, such as the higher quality of information typically found with a librarian's assistance.

Nevertheless, in response to changing conditions, the *Business Case* raised concerns about the agency's ability to continue services in its present form.[17] As such, the report recommended that EPA take the following actions to help facilitate an agencywide dialog regarding the future of the library network:

- survey EPA staff who use the libraries at each location to characterize their needs;
- inventory information resources, including books, journal subscriptions and licenses, databases, and other licensed information as well as library service contracts;
- characterize and assess organizational, business, and technological factors that either enable or constrain services and resources;
- develop models of library services that address the individual needs of participating locations, while leveraging available resources; and
- review the existing policy framework for information resources and develop revisions to address the roles and responsibilities of regional offices, centers, laboratories, and program offices in providing information services to staff.

In addition, federal guidance states that a benefit-cost analysis should be conducted to support decisions to initiate, renew, or expand programs or projects, and that in conducting such an analysis, tangible and intangible benefits and costs should be identified, assessed, and reported.[18] One element of a benefit-cost analysis is an evaluation of alternatives that would consider different methods of providing services in achieving program objectives.

After issuing the *Business Case* report, EPA conducted several assessments of its library network. For example, in its *Optional Approaches* report, EPA provided information to EPA regional management about their options for supporting library services beyond fiscal year 2006. The information and options provided were based on several assessments of the network, such as consultation visits and staff surveys. In addition, some libraries conducted their own assessment of services. For example, after the fiscal year 2007 budget cut was proposed, Region 1 assessed the core library services it provided, library use, and the possible effects of the fiscal year 2007 budget reduction on providing core services and presented a range of options to regional management for consideration.

EPA did not fully complete its assessments, however, before it closed libraries and began to reorganize the network. The assessments were incomplete for the following reasons:

- *EPA did not adequately survey library users to determine their needs.* EPA administered a survey to compare and contrast the relative value of library services across program and regional offices and ascertain the willingness of library users to accept electronic resources and services;

however, only 14 percent of EPA staff responded to the survey. With such a low response rate, EPA could not adequately determine user needs. The survey also did not ask questions that would allow the agency to adequately characterize the needs of library users in reorganizing the library network. In addition, EPA did not attempt to gather views from, or determine the needs of, the public, which is a significant user of EPA libraries.[19] Furthermore, statistics on library use across the network, which EPA relied on, in part, to decide whether and how to reorganize the network, were incomplete and inconsistent.[20] EPA is now developing procedures for keeping complete and accurate use statistics. Such statistics would allow EPA to make more informed decisions regarding the use of its libraries and to determine variation in use on the basis of factors such as where the library is located organizationally, whether it is managed under a separate contract or in combination with related information service functions, or where it is located physically in relation to other publicly accessed areas.

- *EPA did not conduct a complete inventory of libraries' information resources before beginning to close them.* For example, journal subscriptions are a significant cost to the agency, and these subscriptions are duplicated throughout the network. However, EPA did not completely assess duplication and the potential for reducing duplication before beginning to reorganize the network.
- *EPA did not fully characterize and assess organizational, business, and technological factors that would either enable or constrain an optimal level of library services.* For example, EPA did not review, in advance of the library closures, leading practices in digitizing library materials to ensure that such materials are digitized and cataloged correctly. EPA is now undergoing a third-party review of its current digitization standards and procedures, which will inform and serve as a benchmark for the development of EPA's future digitization procedures for library materials. In addition, EPA is relying more on NEPIS to distribute EPA reports electronically, but it only began integrating NEPIS with OLS in late summer 2007 to ensure that hard copy reports digitized in NEPIS are also available through OLS. According to EPA officials, electronic links were established in OLS to all 26,000 reports in NEPIS by the end of December 2007. Many of the electronic reports in NEPIS are born digital and not available in hard copy.
- *EPA did not develop and fully evaluate alternative models of library services that described the benefits, costs, opportunities, and challenges*

of each approach. In its *Optional Approaches* report, EPA describes five different service options: (1) current status—where a library chooses to make no changes to the library operation; (2) network node approach—where a library continues to provide its core services on-site, but purchases or sells some services from or to the library network; (3) liaison approach—where a library greatly reduces or eliminates its physical collection and the labor needed to maintain it with many services purchased from the network; (4) virtual services approach—where a library maintains no library presence on-site, but has a mechanism through which staff can purchase services and resources directly from the network; and (5) deferral of responsibility—where a library ceases all affiliation with the network, forcing staff to procure information services on their own. The report explored the estimated costs associated with each option and recommended a mix of at least three network nodes, three liaison locations, two virtual services locations, and participation of at least one environmental center. However, the alternatives were based on the report's assessment of the regional libraries, rather than on all of the libraries in the network, and it did not explore the benefits, along with the costs, of the various options, including the recommended "mixed" option. Thus, each library had to decide whether it would close without having information on what mix of closed and open libraries would present the most beneficial option and on where to best geographically locate Centers of Excellence or repository libraries.

- *EPA did not, in advance of the reorganization, review the existing policy framework for library resources and develop revisions to this framework to address the roles and responsibilities of regional offices, centers, laboratories, and program offices in providing information services to staff.* Until April 2007, EPA relied on a library policy established in July 1987 that, by 2007, was based on an outdated organizational scheme—the library network under the coordination of an office that did not exist.[21] As we have previously discussed, EPA developed an interim library policy in April 2007, after beginning the reorganization, and is currently developing new library procedures stemming from the policy.

According to EPA officials, EPA decided to reorganize its libraries without fully completing the recommended analyses because it wanted to reduce its fiscal year 2007 funding for the OEI headquarters and regional office libraries by $2 million.[22] However, this claimed savings was not substantiated by any formal

EPA cost assessment. According to EPA officials, the $2 million funding reduction was informally estimated in 2005 with the expectation that EPA would have been further along in its library reorganization effort prior to fiscal year 2007. Furthermore, EPA did not comprehensively assess library network spending in advance of the $2 million estimation of budget cuts. According to OPPTS officials, in December 2005, they decided to close the Chemical Library to expand accessability to library materials through digitization and to achieve related cost savings. Although they planned on closing the Chemical Library at a later date, they moved to close it before the start of fiscal year 2007 because the space was to be reconfigured.[23]

By not completing a full assessment of its library resources and not conducting a benefit-cost analysis of various approaches to reorganizing the network, EPA did not justify the reorganization actions in a way that fully considered and ensured adequate support for the mission of the library network, the continuity of services provided to EPA staff and the public, the availability of EPA materials to a wider audience, and the potential cost savings. In effect, EPA attempted to achieve cost savings without (1) first determining whether potential savings were available and (2) performing the steps that its own study specified as necessary to ensure that the reorganization would be cost-effective.

In: Environmental Protection Agency…
Editor: B. T. Vellios, pp. 33-38
ISBN: 978-1-60692-059-6

Chapter 5

EPA Did Not Fully Inform or Solicit Views from the Full Range of Stakeholders on the Reorganization but Is Now Increasing Its Outreach Efforts

Communicating with and soliciting views from staff and other stakeholders are key components of successful mergers and transformations.[24] We have found that an organization's transformation or merger is strengthened when it makes public implementation goals and a timeline to build momentum and show progress. By demonstrating progress toward these goals, the organization builds staff support for the changes. An organization's transformation and merger is also strengthened when the organization establishes an agencywide communication strategy and involves staff to obtain their ideas, which among other things, involves communicating early and often to build trust, ensuring consistency of message, and incorporating staff feedback into new policies and procedures. Generally, such a strategy helps gain staff ownership for the changes and alleviates uncertainties. Finally, transformations and mergers are strengthened when organizations learn from and use leading practices to build a world-class organization, such as those for library services. However, we found that (1) EPA's August 2006 library plan did not inform stakeholders on the final configuration for the library network or implementation goals and a timeline; (2) EPA lacked an agencywide communication strategy for EPA staff and outside stakeholders, and the extent to which it involved EPA staff and stakeholders to obtain their views was limited; and (3) EPA did not solicit views from industry experts regarding the digitization of library materials and other issues. However, EPA is currently reaching out to both EPA staff and external stakeholders. EPA's communication procedures were limited or inconsistent because EPA acted quickly to make changes in response to a proposed fiscal year 2007 funding reduction, and because of the decentralized nature of the library network.

EPA Did Not Adequately Inform Stakeholders

Through its August 2006 library plan, EPA generally informed internal and external stakeholders of its vision for the reorganized library network, noting that EPA would be moving toward a new model of providing library services to EPA staff and the public, and that this new model would result in a more coordinated library network where more services would be available online. The plan discussed the creation of Library Centers of Excellence and also noted that as a part of the transition to the new library services model, the headquarters, Region 5, Region 6, and Region 7 libraries would close. We found, however, that EPA did not provide sufficient information to stakeholders on how the final library network would be configured or the implementation goals and timeline it would take to achieve this final configuration. More specifically, the plan did not

- inform readers that OPPTS would close its Chemical Library, and that other libraries would reduce their hours of operation or make other changes to their library services;
- provide any detail on which additional libraries would, in an effort to align to the new library service model, change their operations or library collections in the future; and
- inform stakeholders of the intended outcome of the reorganization effort, including what the final configuration of the reorganized library network would look like, and the implementation goals and timeline needed to achieve this final configuration.

OEI officials told us that the purpose of the plan was to provide a framework for how new services would be provided and not for the physical configuration of the network. OEI officials also told us that they were unsure of what the ultimate library model will look like and whether additional libraries would close in the future, since the decision to close is a local decision. Without a clear picture of what EPA intends to achieve with the library network reorganization and the implementation goals and timeline to achieve this intended outcome, EPA staff may not know if progress is being made, which could limit support for the network reorganization.

EPA Lacked an Agencywide Communication Strategy, and the Extent to which It Involved EPA Staff and Stakeholders to Obtain Their Views Was Limited

Because EPA's library structure was decentralized, EPA did not have an agencywide communication strategy to inform EPA staff of, and solicit their views on, the changes occurring in the library network, leaving that responsibility to each EPA library. As a result, EPA libraries varied considerably in the information they provided to staff on library changes. For example, EPA officials from the headquarters and three regional office libraries that closed explicitly informed EPA staff of when the libraries would be closed to physical access. However, EPA officials from the OPPTS Chemical Library did not inform its staff and users of the Chemical Library closure. Rather, these EPA officials informed them that they would be reducing library services and then closed the library without notice or explanation to EPA staff. These officials acknowledge that they could have made a more thorough effort to inform library users about the timing of the library closure. We also found that some of the closed regional libraries informed their staff of the changes occurring at their libraries earlier than the closed headquarters library or other closed regional libraries, and that some libraries communicated changes to their staff more frequently than others. Officials from Regions 5 and 6, for example, began to inform their respective staff of their library closures about 5 months before their libraries closed, whereas officials from Region 7 and headquarters informed their staff of the changes occurring at their libraries only a few weeks prior to their closures. However, we also found that Region 7 officials communicated changes occurring at their library to their staff more frequently after it closed as compared with the other closed regional and headquarters libraries.

The extent to which EPA libraries solicited views from EPA staff also varied by library. Recognizing the decentralized nature of the library network, EPA's *Optional Approaches* report suggested that regional management speak with the unions representing their staff to determine what their staff's library needs are, assure them that changes in the provision of library services would support their needs, and prepare the staff for potential future changes in accessing information resources. However, management in only a few of the regions solicited views from their regional staff through discussions with their unions. According to most of the union representatives we talked with from the libraries that closed, reduced their hours of operation, or changed the way that they provided library services to their users, they were not asked by management to provide their views on the changes that were occurring at their library. At the national level, OEI officials stated that they briefed union representatives on several occasions prior to the reorganization, and that they also provided the union with a draft library plan for review and comment. At the time of our review, EPA had entered into arbitration with the union to resolve the union grievance regarding the reorganization.[25]

Management from only a few of the regional libraries solicited views from their regional science council—an employee group located in each region composed of EPA scientists and technical specialists. For example, officials in Region 1 explained that in an effort to inform management on how best to optimize library services, given the reduction in the budget, management asked its regional science council to poll its scientists, engineers, and technical staff on the library services they most value in the region. In addition, management in Region 5 did not ask the regional science council to provide input on the Region 5 library closure. However, the regional science council in this region submitted a memorandum to management expressing concerns regarding the library closing, and potential impacts the closing would have on the duties performed by EPA scientists and engineers.

In addition, EPA generally did not communicate with and solicit views from external stakeholders, such as the public, before and during the reorganization because the agency was moving quickly to make changes in response to proposed funding cuts. Of the libraries that closed, only the headquarters library informed the public of the changes occurring at its library by posting a notification in the *Federal Register*.[26] The notification informed members of the public on how they could access EPA documents held in the headquarters repository library and or in electronic format. However, the notification was published in the *Federal Register* just 10 days before the library was slated to close and become a repository library. Furthermore, the notification did not provide public users of the library with an opportunity to provide comments on the changes. Rather than publishing a *Federal Register* notice to inform the public of changes or to obtain public views, some of the closed libraries announced the closures to the public through their individual library Web sites after the closures had already occurred. In early 2007, however, we found that EPA's Web site did not include links to the closed regional libraries' Web sites. As a result, members of the public had no way of knowing that the library had closed or of knowing how to access materials that were housed in these libraries.[27]

EPA also did not fully communicate with and solicit views from professional library associations while planning and implementing its library reorganization. EPA did meet with the American Library Association, a professional library association, on a few occasions, but did so later in the reorganization planning process. Furthermore, other professional library associations, such as the Association of Research Libraries, were not consulted at all by EPA officials before or during the library reorganization.[28]

Without an agencywide communication strategy—which involves communicating early and often, ensuring consistency of message, and obtaining views from both EPA staff and external stakeholders—staff ownership for the changes may be limited, and they may be confused about the changes. Furthermore, EPA cannot be sure that the changes are meeting the needs of EPA staff and external stakeholders.

EPA Did Not Solicit the Views of Experts

When developing digitization procedures for library materials, which were noted in the library plan, EPA did not obtain the views of federal experts, such as the Government Printing Office and the Library of Congress, as well as industry experts. These experts could have provided leading practice information and guidance on digitization processes and standards for library materials. As such, EPA cannot be sure that it is using leading practices for library services.

Recognizing the need to communicate with and solicit the views of staff, external stakeholders, and industry experts, EPA has recently increased its outreach efforts. In October 2007, for example, OEI asked local unions throughout the agency to comment on a draft of the 2008 library plan, which includes an overview of EPA's library services for staff and the public and a vision for the future of the EPA library network. Furthermore, since April 2007, OEI has (1) attended and presented information at a stakeholder forum hosted by the American Library Association at which a number of professional library associations—including the American Association of Law Libraries, Special Libraries Association, and Medical Library Association—were present and (2) attended and presented information at a number of professional library association conferences. OEI has also started working with the Federal Library Information Center Committee, a committee managed by the Library of Congress, to develop a board of advisers. This board of advisers—comprising senior library staff at various agencies across the federal sector—is to respond to EPA administrators and librarians' questions about the future direction of EPA libraries. Furthermore, the board of advisers is to serve as one of several experts that EPA can use as sounding boards and informal advisers to help guide the next stages of the library reorganization. Separately, EPA has begun to solicit advice from library experts on procedures EPA is developing for digitization. According to OEI officials, they will ask American Library Association officials and other industry experts to review the procedures before they are made final.

In: Environmental Protection Agency…
Editor: B. T. Vellios, pp. 39-43
ISBN: 978-1-60692-059-6

Chapter 6

EPA Lacks a Strategy to Ensure Continuity of Library Services and Does Not Know whether Its Actions Have Impaired Access to Environmental Information

EPA does not have a strategy to ensure the continuity of library services and does not know the full effect of the reorganization on library services. However, several changes it implemented may have impaired access to library materials and services.

EPA Does Not Have a Strategy to Ensure the Continuity of Library Services

EPA does not have a strategy that ensures the continuation of services to its staff or the public. Based on our review of key practices and implementation steps to assist mergers and organizational transformations, organizations that are undergoing change should seek and monitor staff attitudes and take the appropriate follow-up actions. While EPA's library plan describes the reorganization effort as a "phased approach," it does not provide specific goals, timelines, or feedback mechanisms needed to allow the agency to measure performance and monitor user needs to ensure a successful reorganization while maintaining quality services. The plan recognizes the need to provide training to instruct affected staff on the new services provided, but it does not recognize the need to obtain feedback from library users affected by the changes to identify any concerns they may have in using the new services. EPA has begun to provide training to some staff affected by the reorganization. The agency has also collected staff feedback from some of the libraries; however, such efforts have been random and have not included all of the affected library users nor a statistically valid sample of such users. For example, the Research Triangle Park library solicits feedback from EPA staff on the services provided through the service agreements—and according to EPA officials, the responses so far have been mostly positive; however, the Region 3 library, which also provides services through a service agreement, does not collect such feedback. Without a systematic approach for obtaining feedback from those affected by the reorganization, EPA cannot know whether, or to what extent, the library reorganization has impaired the ability of library users to access environmental information, and if it has impaired their ability, what corrective actions it would need to take to improve services.

To balance the continued delivery of services with merger and transformation activities, it is essential to ensure that top leadership drives the transformation. However, during the reorganization, EPA did not have a national program manager for the library network to oversee and guide the reorganization effort. After the position became vacant in late 2005, it was not filled until May 2007. Without a national program manager for the library network, EPA did not have an official providing an essential level of oversight and guidance that could have ensured that libraries dispersed and disposed of materials properly and in a consistent manner. For example, we found that a universal list of materials available for dispersal from the libraries that were closing was not produced; rather, libraries announced available materials on several different occasions, and the Regions 5 and 6 libraries began dispersing materials prior to the library plan being finalized. In addition, libraries that were closing were not required to develop a list of materials that were to be dispersed or disposed of. Without a program manager in place to consolidate lists of materials to be dispersed and disposed of, some libraries may not have been aware of materials available that could be used for its collection. Because EPA's library plan was unclear and lacked specific procedures and because EPA provided very little oversight, guidance, or control over the reorganization process, it cannot ensure that libraries properly and consistently dispersed or disposed of its library collection, and that library services will continue to be provided to its staff and the public.

EPA Made Several Changes that May Have Impaired the Provision of Materials and Services

Several changes that EPA made to its library network may have impaired the continued delivery of library materials and services to its staff and the public. First, according to EPA's library plan, the agency is moving to deliver more materials and services online. According to EPA estimates, the combined EPA collection in 2003 included 504,000 books and reports; 3,500 journals; 25,000 maps; and 3,600,000 information objects on microfilm. Since the reorganization began, the number of documents in NEPIS increased from 10,700 documents to 26,000, after the unique EPA documents from some of the libraries were digitized and entered into the system. EPA expects to have about 51,000 documents in NEPIS after all hard copy reports are digitized. However, according to EPA officials, because of copyright issues, only unique reports produced by or for EPA will be digitized. Therefore, only about 10 percent of EPA's holdings of books and reports will be available electronically in NEPIS. If the material is not available electronically, EPA staff in locations where libraries have closed will receive the material through an interlibrary loan—delaying access to the materials from 1 day to up to 20 days. According to EPA officials, most interlibrary loan requests are completed in less than 5 days.

Second, with more library materials and services becoming available online, EPA will be relying more on its electronic databases, such as NEPIS and OLS, to identify and distribute library materials. However, EPA has only just recently begun to integrate these systems to allow for easier identification and retrieval of materials that were digitized or that have always been available electronically; nor has it updated these systems to reflect the current location of materials that have been dispersed or disposed of to ensure that staff and the public can identify and receive library materials through them. Although dispersal procedures in EPA's library plan state that the libraries that are closing are responsible for updating OLS, we found that they have not done so. According to EPA officials where libraries had closed, the staff in the receiving libraries were responsible for updating OLS. As a result of such confusion and lack of coordination, for example, all Chemical Library materials still appear as being physically located at the library through OLS, although the library has been closed for over 1 year.

Third, EPA cannot ensure that the service agreements between libraries that had closed and other EPA libraries will be effective. Specifically:

- Only two of the seven service agreements that EPA established were tested in advance to ensure that the services being provided were timely and effective. Even in these cases, EPA did not consider the full range of requests that may be received from the locations planning to close or reduce services. For example, the service agreement between the Cincinnati library and EPA Region 5 was tested for only 4 weeks in 2006, just before the library was to officially close on August 28, 2006. During these weeks, the number of requests made were only 3 percent of the total research and interlibrary loan requests made in Region 5 during fiscal year 2006. This does not provide a realistic assessment of the Cincinnati library's ability to fulfill research requests and interlibrary loans in a timely and effective fashion. Even for this 3 percent, EPA surveyed only a sample of staff to determine their satisfaction with the library services.
- Library materials and services provided under the service agreements are based on a fee-for-service arrangement, which could constrain access to information. For example, due to reduced budgets, prior to the reorganization, OPPTS required management approval of research requests and other service requests. If the agency finds that costs are more than anticipated under the new fee-for-service model, it may require such approvals to try to limit costs. Such actions could limit the research that EPA staff conduct and also delay research efforts. EPA officials have stated that they believe the service agreements provide adequate services and, thus far, believe that they are cost-effective based on preliminary results.
- The Centers of Excellence libraries that provide services to the locations that closed their libraries are all based in the Eastern time zone, which may constrain when services can be provided, especially for EPA staff located in the West.

Although EPA is attempting to continue to meet the needs of its staff, it does not have a plan in place to ensure the continuation of library services for the public, such as state and local government environmental agencies, environmental groups, and other nongovernmental organizations. EPA's library plan stated that the locations where libraries have closed would have a plan to manage public inquiries, and that such locations would refer public requests for information to the public affairs office or program staff.

However, we found that many of the locations where libraries closed have not developed such a plan. In addition, the service agreements with the locations where libraries closed only refer to how services would be provided to EPA staff and not the public.

Finally, EPA may have inadvertently limited access to information because it did not determine whether federal property management regulations applied to the dispersal and disposal of library materials and hence may have disposed of materials that should have been retained. To ensure that federal property is reused to the extent possible, regulations generally require that agencies report surplus property to GSA, which will attempt to find another agency that needs it. If no federal agency needs the property, it may be sold to the public or donated to state or local governments or nonprofit entities. Although agencies may discard property that is subject to the regulations, they must first make a written determination that the property has no value.

While EPA's Fiscal Year 2007 Library Plan included dispersal and disposal criteria and procedures for libraries to follow when deciding on its collections, these criteria and procedures were vague and did not incorporate the federal property regulations. According to a Region 3 EPA official who developed the dispersal and disposal criteria, a clear answer from GSA and from EPA property management officials was not obtained regarding the applicability of federal property management regulations to library materials in the time available before the plan was issued. Furthermore, many of the individual libraries that had dispersed or disposed of library materials did not contact GSA, EPA property management officials, or EPA legal counsel to determine whether federal property management regulations applied, and did not consider the applicability of the federal property management regulations before dispersing or disposing of their library materials. As a result, EPA libraries dispersed and disposed of library materials in a manner inconsistent with federal property management regulations. For example, the Regions 5 and 6 libraries gave materials to private companies, and the OEI headquarters library and the Chemical Library discarded materials without first determining that they had no monetary value. Furthermore, several journal titles from the Chemical Library were disposed of, despite the fact that EPA's Office of Enforcement and Compliance Assurance offered to take the materials and archive them. EPA officials stated that there was lack of clarity regarding whether library materials, such as books and journals, were subject to federal property management regulations. EPA officials stated that they will look into this matter more and will engage federal property management officials at GSA regarding what steps should be taken.

In: Environmental Protection Agency...
Editor: B. T. Vellios, pp. 45-46
ISBN: 978-1-60692-059-6

Chapter 7

EPA PROGRAM OFFICES ARE RESPONSIBLE FOR FUNDING THEIR LIBRARIES AND THEIR REORGANIZATION THROUGH THEIR SUPPORT BUDGETS

The several different program offices responsible for the EPA libraries in the network generally decide how much of their available funding to allocate to their libraries out of larger accounts that support multiple activities. There is no line item for EPA libraries included in the President's budget nor in EPA's more detailed budget justification to Congress. Until fiscal year 2007, library spending had remained relatively stable, ranging from about $7.14 million to $7.85 million between fiscal years 2002 and 2006.[29] OEI, which is the primary source of funding for the regional libraries, typically provides funding for them through each region's support budget, and generally gives regional management discretion on how to allocate this funding among the library and other support services, such as information technology. The regions also obtain a much smaller portion of their library funding from other program offices, such as Superfund, to store and maintain information on the National Priorities List.[30] The extent to which other program offices provide funding to the regional libraries varies.

For the OEI headquarters library and the regional office libraries, however, the approach to library support changed in fiscal year 2007. OEI management decided to reduce library funding by $2 million from $2.6 million in enacted funding in fiscal year 2006 for the OEI headquarters and regional office libraries—a 77 percent reduction for these libraries and a 28 percent reduction in total library funding. After $500,000 of the $2 million reduction was applied to the headquarters library, the regional administrators together decided that the remaining $1.5 million reduction should be spread equally across all regions, rather than by staffing ratios in each region or previous years' spending. However, because it was one of the agencies included in the full-year continuing appropriations resolution for fiscal year 2007, EPA operated near fiscal year 2006 funding levels.

According to EPA, OEI restored $500,000 to the library budget in fiscal year 2007 to support reorganization activities. According to OPPTS officials, while OPPTS did not face a budget cut for fiscal year 2007, it decided to close its Chemical Library nevertheless to improve the library's online services and achieve cost savings.

For EPA staff who had used the libraries that are now closed, EPA has established service agreements with Centers of Excellence. These libraries provide materials and services on a fee-for-service basis charged to the program office whose staff made the request. Funding is provided either as a lump sum to these libraries at the beginning of the fiscal year, which is drawn from as needed, or funding is provided on a monthly basis. The libraries provide monthly reports to the locations being served and coordinate with a liaison at these locations. EPA estimates that services provided under these agreements will cost approximately $170,000 for fiscal years 2007 and 2008.

When planning for the reorganization of the library network, EPA recognized that the responsible dispersal, disposal, and digitization of an EPA library collection is a major project requiring planning, time, and resources. For example, when the relatively small library in Edison, New Jersey, closed in 2004, EPA estimated that it cost $150,000 to disperse 1,000 boxes of materials. EPA did not allocate funds specifically to help the closing libraries manage their collections. According to EPA, the funding for library closures was taken into account during the budget process. As a result, the program or regional office responsible for the library used its usual library funding to pay for closing costs.

The program offices that closed their libraries did not track closing costs, such as boxing and shipping materials. However, EPA estimated that it cost approximately $80,000 to digitize 15,260 titles between December 2006 and January 2007. This cost was paid for by OARM under an already existing contract.

In: Environmental Protection Agency...
Editor: B. T. Vellios, pp. 47
ISBN: 978-1-60692-059-6

Chapter 8

CONCLUSIONS

EPA recognized it needed to ensure that, during and following the reorganization, its library network would continue to provide environmental information to EPA staff and external stakeholders. Accordingly, the agency's reorganization planning identified procedures to follow that would enable the libraries to continue the availability, quality, and timeliness of library materials and services. However, because of a proposed reduction in funding for the OEI headquarters and regional office libraries in fiscal year 2007, EPA did not fully implement these procedures, instead it acted quickly to make changes.

In addition, EPA did not rigorously conduct outreach efforts with EPA staff, external stakeholders, and outside experts, which we have recognized as steps necessary for a successful merger or transformation. As a result, support for the library reorganization may be limited, and staff may be confused about the changes. Furthermore, EPA cannot be sure that the changes are meeting the needs of EPA staff and external stakeholders, and that it is incorporating leading practices for library services and the digitization of materials.

Finally, EPA did not implement best practices that would allow it to measure or monitor the effects of the reorganization or provide oversight of the process, despite EPA having made changes to its library network that may have negatively affected how materials and services are provided to its staff and the public. For example, EPA did not disperse and dispose of library materials in accordance with federal property management regulations or its own procedures and, therefore, may have disposed of materials that are of value and needed for use by staff and the public. Without sufficient monitoring or oversight of the process, EPA cannot be sure of the extent to which the library reorganization has degraded library services, if at all, and therefore cannot take corrective actions if necessary.

In: Environmental Protection Agency…
Editor: B. T. Vellios, pp. 49-50
ISBN: 978-1-60692-059-6

Chapter 9

Recommendations for Executive Action

To ensure that critical library services are provided to EPA staff and other users, we recommend that the Administrator of EPA continue the agency's moratorium on changes to the library network until the agency incorporates and makes public a plan that includes the following four actions:

- Develop a strategy to justify its reorganization plans by (1) evaluating and determining user needs for library services; (2) taking an inventory of EPA information resources and determining the extent to which these resources are used; (3) evaluating technological factors, such as digitization procedures and integration of online databases, to ensure an optimal level of services; (4) evaluating and conducting a benefit-cost assessment for each alternative approach for the network, including the approach that existed before the reorganization; and (5) reviewing and revising, as appropriate, the existing policy and procedures that guide the library network.
- Improve its outreach efforts by developing a process that (1) informs stakeholders of the final configuration of the library network, and the implementation goals and timeline to achieve this configuration; (2) communicates information to stakeholders early, often, and consistently across all libraries, and solicits the views of EPA staff and external stakeholders; and (3) obtains the views of industry experts to determine leading practices for library services.
- Include a process that (1) ensures sufficient oversight and control over the reorganization process, (2) continuously and consistently monitors the

impact of the reorganization on EPA staff and the public, and (3) takes corrective actions as necessary to provide the continued delivery of services.

- Implement procedures that ensure that library materials are dispersed and disposed of consistently and in accordance with federal property management regulations.

In: Environmental Protection Agency…
Editor: B. T. Vellios, pp. 51-55
ISBN: 978-1-60692-059-6

APPENDIX I: OBJECTIVES, SCOPE, AND METHODOLOGY

To review the Environmental Protection Agency's (EPA) library network reorganization, we (1) determined the status of, and plans for, the library network reorganization; (2) evaluated EPA's rationale for its decision to reorganize the library network; (3) assessed the extent to which EPA communicated with and solicited views from EPA staff and external stakeholders in planning and implementing the reorganization; (4) evaluated the steps EPA has taken to maintain the quality of library services following the reorganization, both currently and in the future; and (5) determined how EPA is funding the library network and its reorganization.

We limited our review to the 26 libraries that were part of the EPA library network. According to EPA officials, a library is considered part of the network if its collections are listed in the agency's Online Library System (OLS). Generally, we also conducted the following activities:

- Reviewed relevant EPA documents, plans, policies, guidance, and procedures as well as related laws and requirements pertinent to the library network and the reorganization effort.
- Visited the Office of Environmental Information's (OEI) headquarters library and the Office of Prevention, Pesticides, and Toxic Substances' Chemical Library—both located in Washington, D.C.; the Region 10 library in Seattle, Washington; and the Office of Administration and Resources Management (OARM) library in Cincinnati, Ohio. We visited these libraries because the headquarters library closed physical access to its library space and transitioned into a repository library; the Chemical Library closed physical access to its library space and dispersed and

disposed of its library materials; the Region 10 library reduced its hours of operation; and the OARM library in Cincinnati was identified by EPA as a repository library, a Center of Excellence, and the facility was responsible for digitizing library materials from the closed EPA libraries.

- Interviewed representatives from Lockheed Martin and Integrated Solutions and Services—because these two companies digitized and electronically indexed library materials through already existing contracts with OARM in Cincinnati—and visited a Lockheed Martin facility to observe the digitization process.
- Interviewed EPA librarians, library managers, and program office and regional office managers for the 26 libraries in EPA's library network. When possible, we corroborated information provided to us by EPA officials during the interviews with relevant documentation.

For each of our objectives, some analysis was based on documentation and information provided to us by EPA officials. To the extent possible, we tried to corroborate this information. However, we did not independently verify this information or assess whether it was complete or accurate.

In addition, we conducted work that was specific to each of the report's objectives. To determine the status of and plans for the library network reorganization, we analyzed information that EPA libraries provided to us on the operating status of the libraries as well as materials that have been digitized, dispersed to other EPA and non-EPA libraries, or disposed of as a part of the reorganization effort. We also reviewed drafts and final versions of EPA procedures and criteria for digitizing, dispersing, and disposing of EPA library materials.

To evaluate EPA's rationale for reorganizing the library network, we conducted the following activities:

- Reviewed documents that EPA developed before the reorganization in fiscal year 2007. One of these documents was EPA's 2004 study on the costs and value of EPA's libraries.[31] We did not assess the robustness and adequacy of the methodology and data that EPA used for this study. However, we used this study's recommendations for information on how to further assess and determine the future of the library network to guide our assessment of EPA's subsequent evaluation efforts of the library network. We spoke with a contract official from Stratus Consulting, which helped develop the 2004 study on the costs and value of EPA's libraries, as well as with a researcher from Simmons College who helped conduct an independent review of the study. In addition, we reviewed federal guidelines from the Office of Management and Budget on benefit-cost analyses. We also assessed EPA's survey of library users, examining the adequacy of the response rate of the survey and survey questions. We found the 14 percent response rate to EPA's survey not to be adequate for EPA's purpose because the response rate was low and because EPA did not do any nonresponse analyses to show that those 14 percent who responded were representative of the target population. To determine whether EPA's survey contained questions to adequately characterize the needs of library users in reorganizing the library network, we looked for survey questions that assessed how and how often users used the library space, the library holdings, and the librarian in performing their jobs; the utility of, and satisfaction with, each resource; and to what extent the library materials were available electronically versus in hard copy.

- Asked each of the 26 libraries to provide us with data on the number of walk-ins to the library and other use data between fiscal years 2000 and 2006. We reviewed these data to determine their reliability and sufficiency for EPA to use as a basis for deciding to reorganize the library network. To determine the reliability and sufficiency of EPA's library use data, we checked whether all libraries kept such statistics and whether enough years of data were available to detect a trend in the level of use. We found that not all libraries tracked such library use data and some libraries only kept data for a limited number of years.
- Assessed the National Environmental Publications Internet Site (NEPIS) and OLS to determine the extent of integration between the two systems and to determine how the location of library materials that have been dispersed or disposed of are being updated in OLS.
- Assessed the comprehensiveness of EPA's efforts to evaluate alternative models of library services.

To assess EPA's efforts to communicate with and solicit the views of EPA staff and external stakeholders in planning and implementing the reorganization, we reviewed our past work on key practices and implementation steps to assist mergers and organizational transformations and compared these key practices and implementation steps with EPA's reorganization effort (app. II provides more details on these key practices and implementation steps). More specifically, to determine EPA's efforts to communicate with and solicit input from stakeholders, we reviewed e-mails, notices, and memorandums from EPA library management and program office and regional office management to EPA staff. We also interviewed local union representatives from headquarters and all of EPA's regional offices. Furthermore, we interviewed regional science council representatives from most of the regional offices. The science councils are located in each regional office and consist of EPA scientists and technical specialists. To determine the extent to which EPA communicated with and solicited views from outside stakeholders, we interviewed representatives from several professional library associations and other external stakeholder groups, such as the American Library Association, the Association of Research Libraries, the American Association of Law Libraries, the Special Libraries Association, the Library of Congress' Federal Library and Information Center Committee, and the Union of Concerned Scientists. We also reviewed information that EPA provided to the public via the EPA Web site or, when applicable, *Federal Register* notices.

In evaluating the steps that EPA has taken to maintain the quality of library services following the reorganization both currently and in the future, we reviewed our past work on key practices and implementation steps to assist mergers and organizational transformations and compared these key practices and implementation steps with EPA's reorganization effort (app. II provides more details on these key practices and implementation steps). Furthermore, we reviewed federal property management regulations regarding the dispersal and disposal of federal property, and assessed whether EPA followed these regulations. We also reviewed drafts and final versions of EPA procedures and criteria for dispersing and disposing of EPA library materials. Separately, we determined the possible effects of changes to the library network by (1) determining and evaluating the total number of library materials that would be digitized and made available in NEPIS, and the length of time it would take a user to receive materials via interlibrary loan; (2) evaluating the accuracy of information in NEPIS and OLS; and (3) reviewing and evaluating service agreements between libraries. Finally, we reviewed the roles and responsibilities of the EPA library network management.

To determine funding for the library network and its reorganization, we obtained information on library funding from each of the 26 libraries in the network between fiscal years 2002 and 2007. Because EPA does not specifically track funding for the libraries, the information provided contained a mix of outlays for some fiscal years and budget authority for other fiscal years. In addition, the information provided from each of the libraries only reflected spending by the library and not the source of the funds. For example, a large portion of the funding for the regional office libraries come from OEI, but funding is also received from other EPA program offices, such as Superfund. Furthermore, the funding data received from the libraries contained a mix of funding for contract support; library staff salaries; and acquisition costs for books, journals, and other materials. We interviewed EPA officials to assess data reliability, but we did not independently verify the accuracy and completeness of the data that they provided. After discussions with EPA officials, we decided not to include a table showing funding for each library for fiscal years 2002 through 2007 because of concerns with its reliability. Separately, we interviewed library management from each of the 26 libraries to obtain information on the costs of the reorganization.

We conducted this performance audit from December 2006 through February 2008 in accordance with generally accepted government auditing standards. Those standards require that we plan and perform the audit to obtain sufficient, appropriate evidence to provide a reasonable basis for our findings and conclusions based on our audit objectives. We believe that the evidence obtained provides a reasonable basis for our findings and conclusions based on our audit objectives.

In: Environmental Protection Agency…
Editor: B. T. Vellios, pp. 57-58
ISBN: 978-1-60692-059-6

Appendix II: Key Practices and Implementation Steps for Effective Mergers and Organizational Transformations

Practice	Implementation step
Ensure top leadership drives the transformation.	• Define and articulate a succinct and compelling reason for change. • Balance continued delivery of services with merger and transformation activities.
Establish a coherent mission and integrated strategic goals to guide the transformation.	• Adopt leading practices for results-oriented strategic planning and reporting.
Focus on a key set of principles and priorities at the outset of the transformation.	• Embed core values in every aspect of the organization to reinforce the new culture.
Set implementation goals and a timeline to build momentum and show progress from day one.	• Make public implementation goals and timeline. • Seek and monitor employee attitudes and take the appropriate follow-up actions. • Identify cultural features of merging organizations to increase understanding of former work environments. • Attract and retain key talent. • Establish an organizationwide knowledge and skills inventory to exchange knowledge among merging organizations.
Dedicate an implementation team to manage the transformation process.	• Establish networks to support implementation team. • Select high-performing team members.
Use the performance management system to define responsibility and ensure accountability for change.	• Adopt leading practices to implement effective performance management systems with adequate safeguards.

(Continued).

Practice	Implementation step
Establish a communication strategy to create shared expectations and report related progress.	• Communicate early and often to build trust. • Ensure consistency of message. • Encourage two-way communication. • Provide information to meet specific needs of employees.
Involve employees to obtain their ideas and gain their ownership for the transformation.	• Use employee teams. • Involve employees in the planning and sharing of performance information. • Incorporate employee feedback into new policies and procedures. • Delegate authority to the appropriate organizational levels.
Build a word-class organization.	• Adopt leading practices to build a world-class organization.

Source: GAO.

In: Environmental Protection Agency…
Editor: B. T. Vellios, pp. 59-61

ISBN: 978-1-60692-059-6

APPENDIX III: COMMENTS FROM THE ENVIRONMENTAL PROTECTION AGENCY

UNITED STATES ENVIRONMENTAL PROTECTION AGENCY
WASHINGTON, D.C. 20460

FEB 14 2008

OFFICE OF
ENVIRONMENTAL INFORMATION

Mr. John B. Stephenson
Director
Natural Resources and Environment
United States Government Accountability Office
Washington, DC 20548

Re: EPA Comments on the Government Accountability Office's (GAO) draft report to Congress entitled *EPA Needs to Ensure That Best Practices and Procedures Are Followed When Making Further Changes to its Library Network (GAO-08-304)*

Dear Mr. Stephenson:

This letter provides the U.S. Environmental Protection Agency's (EPA) comments on GAO's draft report entitled *EPA Needs to Ensure That Best Practices and Procedures Are Followed When Making Further Changes to its Library Network (GAO-08-304)*. EPA appreciates the thorough and thoughtful review GAO conducted as well as the opportunity to provide comments on this draft report to Congress.

EPA understands the importance of access to its environmental information and is fully committed to enhancing the EPA National Library Network (Network) to make library information available to a wider audience. The Network model that existed before our efforts began was outdated, having been in existence for more than 30 years. EPA libraries have adopted new technologies over time to support their functions, but much more needed to be done to become a true 21st century operation and a leader among government libraries.

The move to increased electronic delivery of information, the information delivery needs of a customer base working from a myriad of locations, and the growing demands for information and data prompted EPA to re-evaluate its longstanding operational models and move the Network into a new phase that can address current and future needs. These trends have emphasized the need for EPA to identify different ways to operate its libraries while continuing to serve an ever-growing and demanding customer base in a cost-effective manner.

GAO's draft report raises concerns about the process EPA used in making changes to its Network. EPA believes it relied on several previous studies of its Network to inform its decisions. These studies examined a wide range of options and issues, and were supplemented with information on local needs for changes specific to individual libraries. EPA ran a cross-Agency process to carefully consider this information and to obtain input from Agency managers and staff. When implementing changes, EPA staff worked hard to follow best library practices and to meet applicable federal requirements.

We do understand the need to be transparent in our planning around library services. EPA has already taken steps which mirror a number of the GAO recommendations in the draft report. Some of those steps include:

Increased Communication and Outreach

During the past year EPA increased its communication with internal and external stakeholders. EPA has participated in several meetings with professional library associations, including the American Library Association (ALA), Special Libraries Association (SLA), American Association of Law Libraries (AALL), as well as the Union of Concerned Scientists in an effort to get input and share information on Network operations, delivery of services, and plans for the future. EPA will continue these efforts as we develop the strategic direction of the Network.

EPA is also working with the Federal Library and Information Center Committee (FLICC) on EPA plans for the future delivery of library and information access services. FLICC provides advice to federal libraries and information centers in all branches of government, and its mission is to foster excellence in federal library and information services through interagency cooperation. FLICC has identified a board of advisors to work with EPA staff to help address challenges and share collective expertise and experience. The board, whose membership includes representatives from a number of federal libraries, is working with EPA to advise on strategic direction and procedures being developed to support operations within the Network.

We have also provided additional information online about our libraries. In order to provide up-to-date information for people seeking information from EPA libraries, we have updated all Network library web pages to have a consistent design and to provide contact information (http://www.epa.gov/libraries/index.html). We are using these web pages as a mechanism to solicit feedback on current library services and the future direction of the Network. For example, EPA posted information on digitization procedures (http://www.epa.gov/nscep/DigitizationReport.pdf#zoom=100) in an effort to gather feedback.

Enhanced Policy and Procedures

An interim policy for the EPA National Library Network Policy was issued in April 2007, which assigned responsibility for the Network to EPA's Assistant Administrator of the Office of Environmental Information, and established uniform governance and management for the Network. The policy applies to all EPA headquarters and regional offices that provide library services. The final policy will include a number of standard procedures that will be mandatory for all Network libraries. EPA is sharing these procedures with external stakeholders. These Network-wide procedures complement local library procedures that have been in place for a number of years.

Sound Planning for a Strong and Effective Network

EPA is developing a Strategic Plan for the EPA National Library Network and will continue to solicit input from its stakeholders, both internal and external. EPA plans to conduct a needs assessment to inform the strategic planning process. The resulting plan will set overall goals and objectives and a direction for implementation of library services for EPA staff and the public. The plan will recognize the differences in function, the audiences served, and the scope of collections of the libraries in the Network.

Enhance the Network of EPA Libraries

In accordance with report language on the Consolidated Appropriations Act of 2008, EPA is working to ensure on-site support to libraries in EPA Regions 5, 6, and 7, as well as to the Office of Pollution, Prevention, and Toxic Substances (OPPTS) Chemical Library and the Headquarters Library. All these libraries will provide access and services for EPA staff and the public, onsite trained library staff, and a collection of core library materials.

EPA appreciates all the recommendations set forth in the GAO draft report. As we move forward with the modernization of our entire library network, the Agency will prioritize the recommendations made by this draft report.

Let me reassure you that EPA understands the importance of access to its environmental information, values the EPA National Library Network, and recognizes the crucial role it plays in accomplishing the Agency's mission. In addition to these general comments, I have also enclosed a set of specific technical comments. If you would like to discuss these matters further, please contact me at 202-564-6665, or your staff may contact Emma McNamara, Director of the Information Access Division, at 202-566-0655.

Sincerely,

Molly A. O'Neill
Assistant Administrator
and Chief Information Officer

Enclosure

cc: OCIR
OCFO
OPPTS
ARAs

In: Environmental Protection Agency...
Editor: B. T. Vellios, pp. 63-67
ISBN: 978-1-60692-059-6

REFERENCES

[1] At one point, the network included up to 28 libraries.

[2] There is no line item for EPA libraries included in the President's budget proposal, nor is such a line item in EPA's more detailed budget justification to Congress. The $2 million budget reduction for the OEI headquarters library and the regional office libraries was identified in EPA's fiscal year 2007 straw budget, issued on July 8, 2005, out of a total reduction of $10 million for information technology data management under OEI. The Office of Administration and Resources Management also received a reduction in fiscal year 2007 of $1 million for scientific journal subscriptions, but $473,000 of the total was redirected to the Office of Research and Development to continue these journal subscriptions.

[3] A Center of Excellence is another library in the network that provides specific library services to a program office on the basis of its needs. EPA initially referred to these libraries as Centers of Expertise in the 2006 library plan.

[4] Two other repository libraries are managed by the Office of Administration and Resources Management in Research Triangle Park, North Carolina, and Cincinnati, Ohio.

[5] GAO, *Results-Oriented Cultures: Implementing Steps to Assist Mergers and Organizational Transformations*, GAO-03-669 (Washington, D.C.: July 2, 2003).

[6] GAO-03-669.

[7] There are also several libraries and entities at EPA that are not considered part of the network. They include small law libraries located in many of the regions, and entities that are considered resource centers, such as the Water Resources Center. According to EPA officials, these libraries or entities are

not part of the network because their holdings are not cataloged in EPA's Online Library System.

[8] OEI primarily funds these regional office libraries.

[9] U.S. Environmental Protection Agency, Office of Environmental Information, *Business Case for Information Services: EPA's Regional Libraries and Centers*, EPA 260-R-04-001 (January 2004); and *Optional Approaches to U.S. EPA Regional Library Support*, EPA 260-R-05-002 (June 2005).

[10] On September 25, 2007, a ruling by a Federal Labor Relations Authority administrative law judge found that EPA violated federal labor law by failing to enter arbitration with the union regarding the grievance. *U.S. Environmental Protection Agency v. American Federation of Government Employees,* Council 238, No. CH-CA-07-0425 (Sept. 25, 2007). On February 15, 2008, an arbitrator found that EPA had violated provisions of the Master Collective Bargaining Agreement by not engaging the union in impact and implementation bargaining pertaining to the reorganization of its library network. *EPA v. American Federation of Government Employees Council 238*, FMCS Case No. 07-50725 (George Edward Larney, Arbitrator).

[11] These libraries have been designated to be Centers of Excellence for the EPA library network, meaning that these libraries have staff qualified to conduct research in specific areas, have access to tools to support services, and have the ability to handle increased workload. According to EPA officials, the OARM libraries serve as Centers of Excellence for core library services, such as research requests and interlibrary loans, and the Region 3 library serves as a Center of Excellence for business research issues.

[12] In addition, a service agreement was established between the Research Triangle Park library and the National Center for Environmental Assessment in Washington, D.C.

[13] OARM officials in Cincinnati stated that this digitization work was performed by Lockheed Martin, under an already existing contract, and by Integrated Solutions and Services.

[14] Region 5 officials told us that some journal titles were disposed of, but that these materials were disposed of through normal library "weeding" procedures. Weeding is part of a library's regular collection maintenance program, whereby worn, rarely used, or no longer needed titles are identified and disposed of. According to Region 5 officials, they did not keep a list of the journal titles that were disposed of through this process. In addition, officials from the National Vehicle and Fuel Emissions Laboratory

Library noted that they obtained permission from OEI to dispose of about 100 materials that were damaged during a flood in 2007. According to these officials, most of these materials were not used often and are available electronically. This library did maintain a list of the titles that were disposed of.

[15] Pub. L. No. 110-161.

[16] This study only focused on the OEI headquarters library, the 10 regional office libraries, and the OARM libraries located in Cincinnati and Research Triangle Park.

[17] Before the *Business Case* report was finalized, EPA conducted an independent, third-party review of the report. According to the third-party review, the benefit-cost assessment was methodologically sound. However, it found that the report was rooted on a current "as-is," nonstrategic setting and did not provide an empirical, fact-based basis on what might be alternative library service configurations for creating greater value to EPA. As such, the *Business Case* report was found not to address critical questions, such as opportunities for improvements through the centralization of services, changing staffing patterns, or closer alignment with the mission and goals of the agency. According to the third-party review, the *Business Case* report only suggested that the network could be run more efficiently without giving a valid justification as to why or how. In moving forward, the third-party review (1) suggested that, in the long term, EPA should examine ways in which the EPA library services and network can be more closely supported by, and aligned with, the agency's strategic goals and (2) made some specific recommendations on what EPA could do in the short term to more fully evaluate the network and determine alternative models of service.

[18] Office of Management and Budget, *Guidelines and Discount Rates for Benefit-Cost Analysis of Federal Programs*, OMB Circular A-94 (Washington, D.C.: Oct. 29, 1992).

[19] According to EPA estimates, 20 to 40 percent of the reference requests received by regional libraries are from the public.

[20] EPA has reported that a significant drop in walk-ins to the libraries was a major factor in deciding to reorganize the library network and establish a more virtual approach to providing library materials and services. However, a review of walk-in statistics and other use statistics reveals that some libraries did not keep complete statistics. For example, Regions 4 and 6 did not keep statistics on the number of walk-ins, and several other libraries did not keep these statistics prior to 2003. For the regional libraries that did

keep track of the number of walk-ins, these statistics showed that walk-ins had decreased only 18 percent from 2003 through 2006; ranging from a decrease of 83 percent in Region 5 to an increase of 66 percent in Region 10.

[21] The position of national program manager for the EPA library network was located within the Information Services Branch of the Information Management and Services Division, Office of Information Resources Management—a predecessor to OEI.

[22] The $2 million cost savings for the libraries was included in the President's fiscal year 2007 budget proposal for EPA. However, like most agencies, EPA was included in the full-year continuing resolution, which held appropriations near fiscal year 2006 levels.

[23] Nearly half of the space in the Chemical Library is occupied by shelving units. Because the space and the shelving are considered to be historical, EPA cannot remove the shelves. The rest of the space has been converted to cubicles.

[24] See GAO-03-669. This report identified nine key practices and related implementation steps that have led to successful mergers and transformations in large private and public sector organizations. Since all nine key practices and implementation steps could help guide EPA's library reorganization effort, we have included this information in appendix II.

[25] In September 2007, the national EPA union held arbitration talks with EPA. The EPA union won its unfair labor practice claim against the agency. More specifically, the Federal Labor Relations Authority administrative law judge ruled that EPA violated federal labor law by failing to enter arbitration with the union regarding its grievance about the library restructuring. *U.S. Environmental Protection Agency v. American Federation of Government Employees*. The ruling also required the agency to post signs notifying employees that EPA had violated labor law. On February 15, 2008, an arbitrator found that EPA had violated provisions of the Master Collective Bargaining Agreement by not engaging the union in impact and implementation bargaining pertaining to the reorganization of its library network. *EPA v. American Federation of Government Employees Council 238*, FMCS Case No. 07-50725 (George Edward Larney, Arbitrator).

[26] 71 Fed. Reg. 54,986 (Sept. 20, 2006).

[27] EPA has since revised its Web site to include links to the closed EPA libraries. The individual library Web sites for the closed libraries direct library users to EPA online resources, such as OLS and NEPIS, or to the library with which they have established a service agreement.

[28] The Association of Research Libraries has developed a library assessment tool—called LibQUAL+—that allows libraries to measure and report on library service quality.

[29] These figures are based on estimates from EPA. We did not independently determine their accuracy. Because EPA does not track library funding, each library in the network provided estimates that were based on past spending and enacted funding. However, libraries may have varied in the type of spending data provided in terms of whether the data included contract costs, salaries, and acquisitions.

[30] The National Priorities List is EPA's list of the most dangerous hazardous waste sites in the country.

[31] U.S. Environmental Protection Agency, Office of Environmental Information, *Business Case for Information Services: EPA's Regional Libraries and Centers*, EPA 260-R-04-001 (January 2004).

INDEX

A

B

C

D

E

F

G

H

I

J